the Girls' Summer book

PSS!

PRICE STERN SLOAN

An Imprint of Penguin Group (USA) Inc.

Written by Ellen Bailey

Illustrated by Nellie Ryan and Lisa Jackson

Cover illustrated by Nikalas Catlow

Use common sense at all times—always wear appropriate safety gear, be very careful with scissors, and be considerate of other people.

PRICE STERN SLOAN
Published by the Penguin Group
Penguin Group (USA) Inc., 375 Hudson Street, New York, New York 10014, USA
Penguin Group (Canada), 90 Eglinton Avenue East, Suite 700,
Toronto, Ontario M4P 2Y3, Canada
(a division of Pearson Penguin Canada Inc.)
Penguin Books Ltd., 80 Strand, London WC2R 0RL, England
Penguin Group Ireland, 25 St. Stephen's Green, Dublin 2, Ireland
(a division of Penguin Books Ltd.)
Penguin Group (Australia), 250 Camberwell Road, Camberwell, Victoria 3124, Australia
(a division of Pearson Australia Group Pty. Ltd.)
Penguin Books India Pvt. Ltd., 11 Community Center,
Panchsheel Park, New Delhi—110 017, India
Penguin Group (NZ), 67 Apollo Drive, Rosedale, North Shore 0632, New Zealand
(a division of Pearson New Zealand Ltd.)
Penguin Books (South Africa) (Pty.) Ltd., 24 Sturdee Avenue,
Rosebank, Johannesburg 2196, South Africa
Penguin Books Ltd., Registered Offices:
80 Strand, London WC2R 0RL, England

ISBN 978-0-8431-9853-9   10 9 8 7 6 5

CONTENTS

PICNIC PERFECTION

Add some glamour when you plan a perfect picnic.

FABULOUS FLOWERS

To make these beautiful folded lotus flowers, all you'll need are some square napkins—it doesn't matter whether they are made of paper or fabric.

I. Open the napkin and spread it flat. Fold each corner of the napkin into the center, as shown below. You will now have a small square.

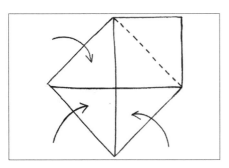

2. Fold each corner of the new square into the center. You will now have an even smaller square.

3. Turn the napkin over, and again fold each corner into the center.

4. Hold the center of the napkin with one hand. Use your other hand to reach underneath the napkin and pick up one of the folded bottom corners.

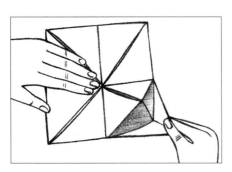

5. Pull the bottom corner up and out to create a petal. You'll need to push the top corner into the middle of the petal. Repeat for each corner.

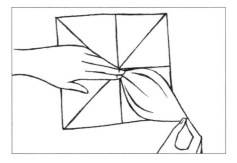

6. You will now have a flower shape. Keeping hold of its center, reach underneath again and pick up one of the folded-in bottom corners from the inner layer. Pull it up and out to create a smaller petal.

7. Repeat for each of the four folded-in corners. You now have a beautiful lotus flower!

SUMMER SNAPS

Can you figure out which girl took each of the photos below at this summer party?

You'll need to think about where each photographer is standing and which girl she is aiming her camera at. Check your answers on page 92.

A

B

C

D

E

F

PICTURE THIS

Use the grid lines to help you draw your own version of this picture in the bigger grid below.

EAGLE EYES

Who will be the first of your family or friends to find each of the items below?

Write that person's initials in the box next to the item. The winner is the person who finds the most. You might be able to find everything listed on a long car ride, or it might take you all summer.

WHAT CAN YOU FIND?

1. Traffic lights		16. A bakery	
2. A train station		17. A white van	
3. Someone wearing red		18. A supermarket	
4. A dog		19. A taxi	
5. A police car		20. An airplane	
6. A hair salon		21. A bookstore	
7. A bus stop		22. A museum	
8. A bridge		23. A clothesline	
9. A truck		24. A convertible	
10. Someone taking photos		25. Someone using a phone	
11. Someone on roller skates		26. A restaurant	
12. A tent		27. Someone wearing a uniform	
13. A baby		28. A cinema	
14. Flowers		29. A candy store	
15. A phone booth		30. A fire engine	

HEAD-TO-TOE SUMMER BEAUTY

Whether you're heading off to the beach on your summer vacation or spending it at home, get ready to shine with these make-and-use summer beauty products.

HEALING HAIR WRAP

Sunshine, salt water, and chlorine can all dry out your hair and leave it looking dull and strawlike, so try out this moisturizing conditioning treatment to restore shine.

First, warm a towel in the dryer. Next, wash your hair and apply a thick layer of conditioner before wrapping it in the hot towel. Leave for ten minutes. During this time, use a hair dryer to warm your hair through the towel. Rinse, dry, and then show off your gorgeous, silky locks!

HEAVENLY HONEY AND OATMEAL FACE MASK

Soothe sun-kissed skin with this cooling face mask. Mix one tablespoon of plain yogurt with one tablespoon of oatmeal and a few drops of honey.

Apply a thick layer to your face, avoiding the skin around your eyes, and leave for ten minutes. Rinse with warm water, then apply a thick layer of moisturizer. Your face will now feel soothed and ready for another day in the sun.

SWEET SKIN BODY SCRUB

Relieve dry skin and remove dead skin cells with this delicious body scrub.

Pour two tablespoons of granulated sugar into a bowl. Add the juice of half a lemon and four tablespoons of olive oil. Massage the mixture into your skin, then rinse off in a warm bath before bedtime. Pat your skin dry before getting into bed.

When you wake up in the morning, the remaining olive oil on your skin will have soaked in, making your skin feel sumptuously smooth.

GLITTER LIP GLOSS

You can dazzle on a summer's day simply by adding a flash of glitter. Find an old lipstick and scoop out the leftover color into a bowl. Add some petroleum jelly and some craft glitter. Leave in the sunshine until it starts to melt.

Using a metal teaspoon, blend the mixture together. Scoop the mixture into the old lipstick case, then place in the fridge to set. After one hour, dab some on your lips to complete your sparkly summer style.

REFRESHING LIME AND MINT FOOT SOAK

Walking around barefoot or in sandals can cause the skin on your feet to become rough. To soften up your feet, prepare a refreshing foot soak by putting ten mint leaves in a large bowl.

Chop a lime into quarters (ask an adult to help you with this), add to the bowl, and use the back of a spoon to crush everything together.

Fill a clean basin with warm water and add the lime and mint mixture. Soak your feet for fifteen minutes until soothed and refreshed. Pat them dry with a clean towel and apply moisturizer. Your feet will now feel soft and smooth again.

WHICH SUMMER GODDESS ARE YOU?

Follow this funky flowchart to find out.

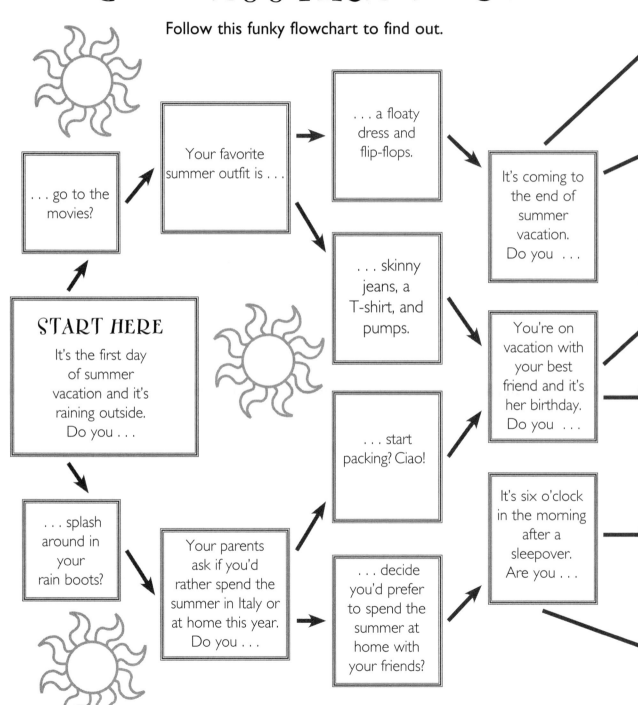

... go to the movies?

Your favorite summer outfit is ...

... a floaty dress and flip-flops.

... skinny jeans, a T-shirt, and pumps.

It's coming to the end of summer vacation. Do you ...

You're on vacation with your best friend and it's her birthday. Do you ...

START HERE
It's the first day of summer vacation and it's raining outside. Do you ...

... splash around in your rain boots?

Your parents ask if you'd rather spend the summer in Italy or at home this year. Do you ...

... start packing? Ciao!

... decide you'd prefer to spend the summer at home with your friends?

It's six o'clock in the morning after a sleepover. Are you ...

... make the most of relaxing in your backyard?

... try to fit in as many fun activities as possible?

... plan to go to a theme park she's been talking about?

... invite all your close friends over for a fancy party?

... already getting ready for a fun-filled day?

... tired because you stayed up talking most of the night before?

YOU ARE HEMERA, GODDESS OF SUNSHINE

You love the long summer days and adore playing outside in the sunshine. Complete your goddess look with a sun-shaped hair clip and a yellow ribbon.

YOU ARE AESTAS, GODDESS OF SUMMER

You're bursting with energy. Your friends love that you're full of exciting ideas of things to do and places to visit. Complete your goddess look by pinning braids of grass into your hair.

YOU ARE IRIS, GODDESS OF RAINBOWS

You love to travel, and summer vacation gives you the chance to visit new places and meet new people. Make a necklace of rainbow-colored beads to complete your goddess look.

YOU ARE ANTHEIA, GODDESS OF FLOWERS

You are a chilled-out girl who likes spending time at home with your friends over summer vacation. You appreciate the beauty of summer. Pin some fresh flowers in your hair to complete your goddess look.

STEP IT UP FOR SUMMER

When the sun is shining and you feel like dancing, why not create your very own summer dance routine?

PUT ON YOUR DANCING SHOES

To get started, slip on some comfortable clothes—sweatpants, a T-shirt, and your favorite sneakers are ideal. Take a portable music player outside and turn on your favorite dance track. Now you are ready to try these sassy dance moves. You can create your own cool routine by mixing up the moves below in whichever order you choose. Once you've got the hang of it, why not have a competition with your friends and battle it out to see who's got the best moves? You can even throw your own signature dance move into the mix!

Dime Stop	Wave 1	Wave 2

Dance around, then suddenly stop. Wait two beats, then continue dancing.

Move your whole body as if a wave of motion is passing through you. This move looks really good if you do it with a friend. Stretch your arms out to either side, and make the wave travel from fingertip to fingertip, as above.

The Robot

Dance using stiff, precise movements—as if you're a robot.

The Swag

Sway your arms in time to the music while walking in place.

Drop It

With your hands above your head, bend your knees and drop all the way to the floor, then "pop" back up without pausing.

Pop-Lock Walk

Imagine your arms and legs are connected with string so that when you lift your right arm up, your right leg also lifts, and vice versa.

Heel-Toe Flick

Bend your knees and turn your feet out so that your heels are facing each other. On the next beat of the music, turn your feet in so the toes are now facing each other.

Running Girl

Run in place while bending your arms up to your chest. As you run, straighten your arms out in front of you in time to the music.

IT'S CAKE O'CLOCK!

Sunny summer days are the best time to hang out with friends.
Keep reading to learn how to throw the perfect party.

CUTE CUPCAKES

Cute cupcakes are great party food. Here's how to bake up a batch:

You will need:

For the batter: 2 eggs • 1/2 cup sugar • 1/2 cup self-rising flour • 1/2 cup butter at room temperature • 18 to 20 cupcake pan liners • **For the icing:** 1/2 cup powdered sugar • 1/4 cup butter at room temperature • chocolate chips, sprinkles, etc.

1. Turn the oven on to 350°F. Be sure to ask an adult for help.

2. Place the cake ingredients into a large mixing bowl and stir with a wooden spoon until you have a smooth mixture.

3. Arrange your cupcake pan liners over two muffin tins—this mixture makes 18 to 20 cupcakes. Put two teaspoons of mixture into each liner.

4. Ask an adult to bake the cupcakes in the oven for 10 to 15 minutes, or until they are golden brown on top.

5. Ask an adult to help you take the cupcakes out of the oven and place them on a wire rack to cool.

6. Put the powdered sugar and butter into a bowl and stir until smooth.

7. Use a knife to spread the icing on the top of each cupcake. Decorate with chocolate chips, sprinkles, or whatever you like!

CAKE STAND PERFECTION

To add a touch of elegant sophistication to your party, why not make a cake stand to present your cute cupcakes on? Here's how:

You will need:

3 party cups (paper or plastic) • a sharp pencil • a blob of modeling clay • 10 feet of gift ribbon • scissors • 2 small party plates • 1 large party plate • adhesive tape

1. Position a cup on top of the modeling clay. Push the tip of the pencil through the middle of the cup base into the clay to make a small hole.

2. Do the same to the other two cups and the three plates. Discard the clay.

3. Cut the ribbon into two equal lengths.

4. Holding the ends together, thread them through the hole in one cup, as shown below.

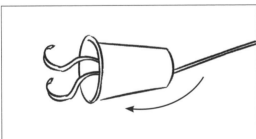

5. Thread the ribbons through the top of the small plate and then through the bottom of the second cup.

6. Now thread the ribbons through the top of the other small plate and then through the bottom of the last cup.

7. Thread both the ribbon ends through the top of the large plate and secure the ends to the bottom of the final plate with tape, as shown below.

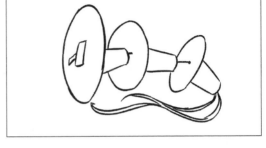

8. Hold the ends of the ribbon onto the first cup in one hand and sit the cake stand down on its base with the other hand. Carefully tie the ribbon ends in a knot and finish with a bow.

9. Arrange the cupcakes on the cake stand.

Now all you need to do is plan the perfect party. Turn the page to find out how.

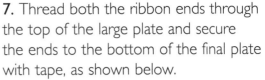

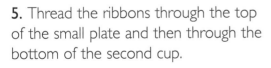

SUMMER PARTY PLANS

Throwing a party takes planning. Follow the advice below
to ensure your party day runs perfectly.

Send invitations. Choose some friends to invite to your party. Decide when and where you plan to hold the party, and then fill in the invitations on the opposite page. Cut out each one and color them in before handing them out to your friends.

Choose a menu. As well as baking cute cupcakes to serve (see pages 14–15), afternoon party foods also include dainty sandwiches and cookies.

Choose a color scheme. Choose two colors that go well together—for example, pink and blue or yellow and green. Pick a tablecloth to match your color scheme and choose napkins in a contrasting color.

Find flowers. Place a vase of flowers that work with your color scheme in the center of the table.

Be the hostess with the mostest. As your guests arrive, show them to the table and ask them to take a seat.

Prepare drinks. Try making a delicious "watermelonade" drink. (See page 82 for a refreshing recipe.) Serve in pretty teacups with matching saucers.

Once everyone has a drink and some food, take off your apron and join the party!

PRETTY PARTY INVITATIONS

Fill in the details on the invitation cards below, then carefully cut them out.

The letters *RSVP* appear at the bottom of each invitation—this is short for the French phrase "répondez s'il vous plaît," which means "please would you reply."

Dear: ....
You are invited to a summer party hosted by:
....
Location: ....
Date and Time: ....
RSVP

Dear: ....
You are invited to a summer party hosted by:
....
Location: ....
Date and Time: ....
RSVP

Dear: ....
You are invited to a summer party hosted by:
....
Location: ....
Date and Time: ....
RSVP

Dear: ....
You are invited to a summer party hosted by:
....
Location: ....
Date and Time: ....
RSVP

Dear: ....
You are invited to a summer party hosted by:
....
Location: ....
Date and Time: ....
RSVP

Dear: ....
You are invited to a summer party hosted by:
....
Location: ....
Date and Time: ....
RSVP

Color in each invitation before passing them
out to your friends.

PICNIC PUZZLE

The girls have made a list of some of the food at
their picnic, but two of their items are wrong.

They think that there are:
5 cheese slices, 5 cupcakes, 4 croissants,
6 watermelon slices, and 10 strawberries.
How many of each can you see?
Check your answers on page 92.

TRAVEL TRIVIA

Test your friends' knowledge with this fun quiz. Use the scorecard opposite to fill in your answers, check to see if they're right on page 92, and find out who is the best at travel trivia.

1. In which city would you find the River Seine?

A. Madrid

B. Berlin

C. Paris

D. New York

2. What is special about Italy's Tower of Pisa?

A. It's the tallest tower in the world.

B. It's leaning over.

C. There is a pizza restaurant at the top.

D. You can see it from space.

3. Which of the following names are you not allowed to call a pig in France?

A. Bill

B. Napoleon

C. Simon

D. Vince

4. In which country would you find the deadly funnel-web spider?

A. Iceland

B. France

C. Australia

D. United Kingdom

5. What would happen if you jumped into Israel's Dead Sea?

A. You'd freeze.

B. You'd sink.

C. You'd float.

D. You'd be surrounded by sharks.

6. What is the basic unit of currency in China?

A. Yuan

B. Yan

C. Yen

D. Yin

7. In Chile, it's rude to show someone an open palm with the fingers separated. It means you think they are . . .

A. ugly

B. greedy

C. lazy

D. stupid

8. Which of the following isn't one of the Seven Wonders of the Ancient World?

A. The Great Pyramid of Giza

B. The Hanging Gardens of Babylon

C. The Temple of Achilles at Ephesus

D. The Statue of Zeus at Olympia

9. What are Niagara Falls?

A. Waterfalls

B. Mountains

C. Pyramids

D. Oceans

11. On which continent is the Amazon Rainforest?

A. Asia

B. Africa

C. South America

D. Europe

10. Which of these is a beach in Sydney, Australia?

A. Bondi Beach

B. Mouldy Beach

C. Fungi Beach

D. Tripod Beach

12. On which continent is the South Pole?

A. Europe

B. Antarctica

C. Africa

D. North America

	Player 1	Player 2	Player 3	Player 4
1				
2				
3				
4				
5				
6				
7				
8				
9				
10				
11				
12				
Total				

SURF'S UP!

Everybody's gone surfing. Grab your board and join in with these surf activities.

POP-UP ON YOUR BOARD

Don't let a lack of waves to ride bother you. If you are a true surfer girl, you can perfect a surfing technique called a "pop-up" whether you're on the beach or in your bedroom. Here's how:

1. Place a towel on the floor and fold it lengthwise.

2. Lie on your stomach along the towel, and paddle your arms as though you're swimming your board through the water.

3. When you're ready to catch a wave, place your palms flat on the towel underneath your shoulders. Keeping your body straight, use your arms to do a full push-up, as shown below.

4. Pull your knees toward your stomach, hop onto your feet, and stand up with one foot in front of the other on the "board." This is called a "pop-up."

The pop-up should be one swift, smooth motion straight to a standing position. So keep practicing until you're a superconfident surfer girl.

SURFER GIRLS

A. How many girls have bikinis?

B. How many have wet suits?

C. How many have only one foot on their board?

D. How many have ponytails?

Check your answers on page 92.

SUMMER SCIENCE

Turn your house into a laboratory with these exciting experiments.

HOW TO BRING A PAPER FISH TO LIFE

"Surface tension" is a property of all liquids. It is a bit like a layer of skin on top of the liquid. It is the reason that water collects in droplets and why small insects can walk on the surface of lakes and rivers. Conduct this science experiment to see the effects of surface tension in action.

Start by cutting out some fish from paper—trace the template of the fish opposite to make each one.

Next, fill a bowl with water and place the paper fish flat on the surface.

Take a bottle of dishwashing liquid and squeeze a small drop behind the tail of each fish. The soap will break the surface tension of the water, causing the fish to swim away quickly.

HOW TO MAKE A RAINBOW

Sunlight is made up of all the colors of the rainbow, and when it passes through water it splits up into light waves of different lengths, which we see as different colors. You can catch these light waves by standing a mirror in a plate of water on a table in front of a window.

Wait for a day when the sun is streaming through your windows for this experiment. Move the mirror around until the light passes through the water and bounces off the mirror, making a rainbow appear on the wall.

WRITE TO ME

Fill in your details on these cards. Cut them out and give them
to the friends you make over the summer so you never lose touch.

Name: ....
Address: ....
....
E-mail: ....

Name: ....
Address: ....
....
E-mail: ....

Name: ....
Address: ....
....
E-mail: ....

Name: ....
Address: ....
....
E-mail: ....

Name: ....
Address: ....
....
E-mail: ....

Name: ....
Address: ....
....
E-mail: ....

Color in each card
before you give it away.

CRACK THOSE CODES

You find four bottles washed up on the beach. Three of them contain riddles written in secret codes, and the fourth contains cryptic clues that will help you crack the codes.

Match each clue to the correct bottle, decipher the messages, then figure out the answers to the riddles. Answers are on page 92.

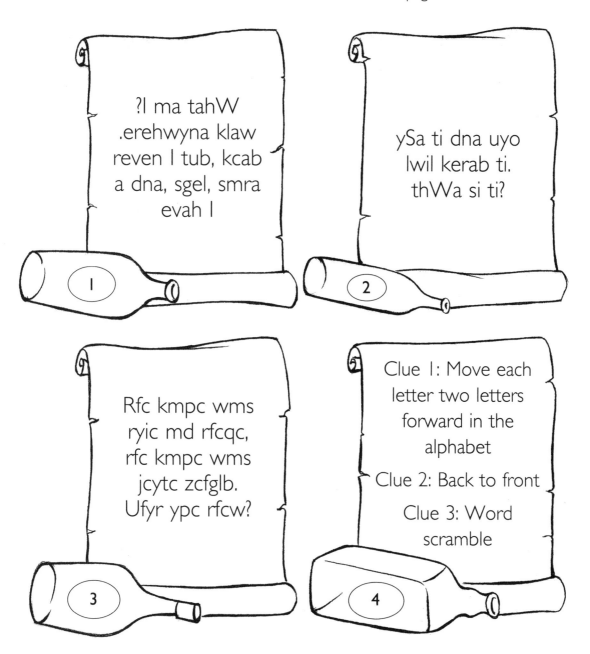

1

?I ma tahW
.erehwyna klaw
reven I tub, kcab
a dna, sgel, smra
evah I

2

ySa ti dna uyo
lwil kerab ti.
thWa si ti?

3

Rfc kmpc wms
ryic md rfcqc,
rfc kmpc wms
jcytc zcfglb.
Ufyr ypc rfcw?

4

Clue 1: Move each letter two letters forward in the alphabet

Clue 2: Back to front

Clue 3: Word scramble

RAINY-DAY DECISIONS

Don't let the rain get you down. This fortune teller contains lots of great ideas for how to fill the time if you're stuck inside!

HOW TO MAKE IT

1. Cut out the fortune teller on the opposite page. Fold one corner over to the other to make a triangle so that the writing is on the outside.

2. Fold your triangle in half again to form a smaller triangle. Then unfold the sheet and lay it flat.

4. Turn the fortune teller over and repeat step three, folding the new corners into the middle.

5. Fold the fortune teller in half from edge to edge, so the colors remain on the outside.

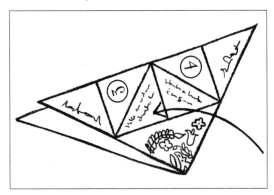

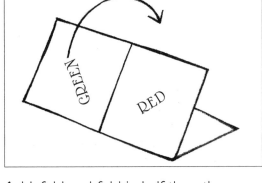

3. Fold each corner of the sheet into the middle so the corners all meet at the center of the sheet.

6. Unfold and fold in half the other way.

7. Slide the thumb and forefinger of both hands under the flaps of the fortune teller, and find your fortune!

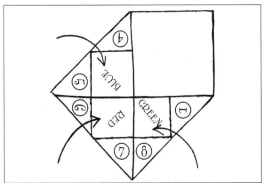

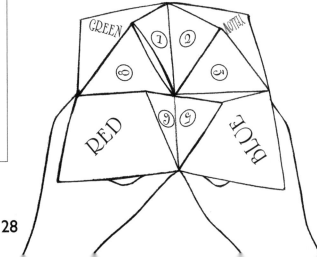

BLUE

RED

YELLOW

GREEN

5 — Give each other makeovers.

6 — Make a treasure hunt for your friends.

4 — Write a letter to a friend.

7 — Put on a play.

3 — Make an indoor obstacle course and time each other to complete it.

8 — Make a family "newspaper" of what's happened this summer so far.

2 — Play charades, acting out places you've been or things you've seen this summer.

1 — Create outfits from your closet and perform a fashion show.

WHAT TO DO NEXT

Now ask someone to choose a color from the outside flaps. Spell out the color, opening and closing the fortune teller for each letter. Holding the fortune teller open, ask your friend to pick one of the numbers shown inside. Count out the number and ask them to pick another one. Open up the flap beneath that number to reveal a rainy-day activity.

Fill the back of your fortune teller with flowers.

JOKE CORNER

Why is the sand wet?
Because the sea weed.

How does a mermaid travel around?
On an octobus.

Why were the elephants thrown
out of the swimming pool?
Because their trunks kept falling down.

What do you call a wicked old woman
who lives by the sea?
A sandwich.

VACATION STYLE QUIZ

Everyone looks forward to different things about summer vacation.
Take this quiz to see what kind of vacationer you are.
Find out what your answers mean on the next page.

1. If you could take only one item on vacation with you, what would it be?

A. Magazine

B. Camera

C. Sunglasses

D. Beach ball

2. Which item of clothing would you be most annoyed to forget?

A. Sarong

B. Favorite T-shirt

C. Expensive new skirt

D. Swimsuit

3. What is the first thing you do when you arrive at your destination?

A. Get an ice cream

B. Flick through a guidebook

C. Hit the local shops

D. Go swimming

4. Which type of shoes do you spend most of your vacation wearing?

A. Flip-flops

B. Sandals

C. High heels

D. Sneakers

5. What is your favorite vacation drink?

A. Milkshake

B. Bottled water

C. Fruit smoothie

D. Energy drink

6. How will you spend the last day of your vacation?

A. Relaxing on a deck chair

B. Dashing to all the sights you haven't seen yet

C. At the theater

D. Playing soccer with a new group of friends

WHAT YOUR ANSWERS MEAN

Count up how many times you chose each letter and then look at the results below to find out what your answers say about you. If you got an even mix of letters, then you're a girl who likes to try a bit of everything on vacation.

MOSTLY As:
LAID-BACK LADY

When you're on vacation, your aim is to kick back and relax. You love lounging by the pool, indulging in long, lazy lunches, and flicking through magazines.

A week or two of this will leave you feeling totally chilled, but make sure you don't miss out on the fun because you've fallen asleep!

MOSTLY Cs:
CITY STAR

You're a sophisticated girl who enjoys visiting new cities and taking in the culture. You always look superstylish and love shopping and dining in posh restaurants.

Don't forget that even the most glamorous of girls need some downtime, so make sure you leave time to pull on some comfy clothes and unwind.

MOSTLY Bs:
SASSY SIGHTSEER

You're never seen without your camera and love visiting famous landmarks. The more you can find out about your destination before you go, the more you'll get out of it. So grab that guidebook and get investigating.

MOSTLY Ds:
ACTIVE ADVENTURER

Always the first to suggest a game of beach volleyball or Frisbee, you're a sporty chick who loves to stay active.

Exercise is a great way to relax and have fun on vacation and will help keep you fit and healthy, too.

What can you see from your window?

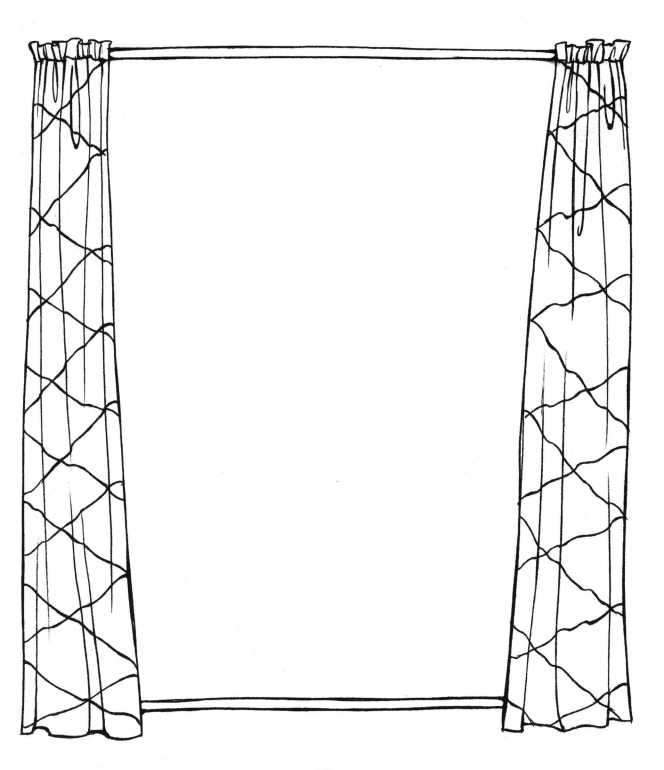

WATER WORLD

Complete the puzzles and turn to pages 92–93 to check your answers.

Which swimmer will come out of which chute?

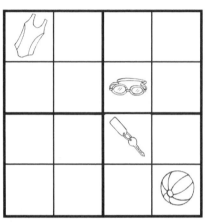

Complete the grid above so that each column, each row, and each of the four larger squares contains only one swimsuit, a beach ball, a locker key, and a pair of goggles.

Using only three straight lines, divide the swimming pool into six sections with one swimmer and one beach ball in each.

Can you spot two identical burgers in this diner?

Can you find a clear path for this girl through the maze to the jacuzzi?

LUXURY LUGGAGE

Make sure your luggage is instantly recognizable and the most stylish in town with this fabulous oversize luggage tag.

1. Cut a large rectangle (that measures about half the size of this page) from a thick piece of cardboard (an old cereal box will do). Cut off the top and bottom corners of one side to make your tag shape. Use the point of a pencil to make a hole at one end of it—this will be the hole through which you can thread a ribbon to tie it to your bag.

2. Cut out enough paper to cover one side of your tag, and stick it on with glue. Write your name, address, and telephone number on it. This way, if your luggage gets lost, the person who finds it will be able to return it to you. You could decorate this side with felt-tip pens and maybe even some glitter or sequins to make it really eye-catching.

3. During your trip, collect paper souvenirs such as ticket stubs, museum brochures, information pamphlets, postcards, sketches, maps, menus, interesting food packaging, and stickers. Sort through the items you have collected and cut out pictures or words that look good and remind you of your vacation.

4. Cover the reverse side of your luggage tag with white glue (dilute the glue with water if it's very thick). Stick the pictures on, then cover them with another layer of glue.

5. When the glue has dried and the surface of your tag looks shiny, thread a piece of brightly-colored ribbon or string through the hole and tie it onto the handle of your bag.

FIND THE FASHIONISTAS

Can you find the two girls below in the crowd? Answers are on page 93.

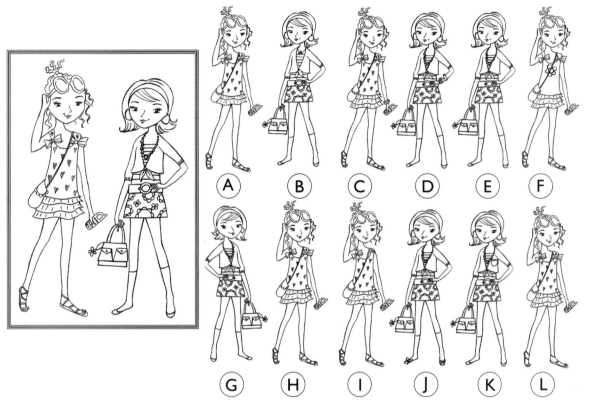

A B C D E F

G H I J K L

Decorate these flip-flops.

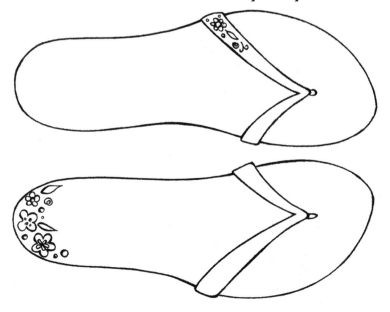

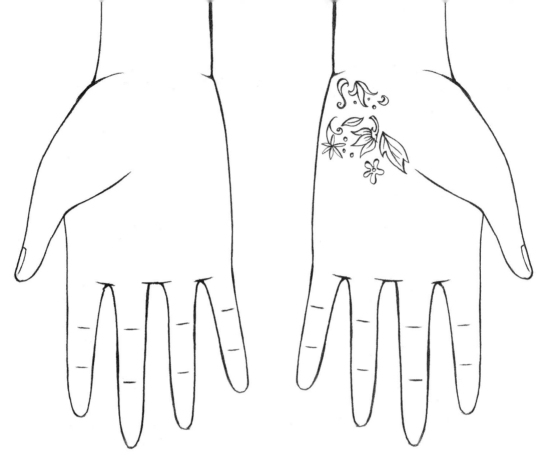

Can you decorate these hands with henna?

RELAXATION STATION

**Stay cool and calm this summer with these yoga moves
that stretch tired muscles.**

Sit with your bottom close to the front of your chair. Take three
deep breaths, then perform these two moves.

Sunshine Stretch: Tuck your left foot underneath the chair and slide your right foot forward as far as it will go. Keeping your back straight and your left arm by your side, breathe in as you stretch your right arm up in front of you. Breathe out as you lower your arm, then repeat three times with each arm.

Chair Cat: Sit with your feet flat on the floor and your hands on your thighs. Stretch your body up and backward so that you're looking at the ceiling, breathing out as you do so.

Now breathe in as you lean forward over your knees and stretch the back of your neck. Repeat five times.

PINK POMEGRANATE PUDDING

Pomegranate seeds look like beautiful pink jewels, and you can buy this delicious fruit in most supermarkets.

To make a pretty, pink pomegranate pudding that'll bring the feeling of summer into your dining room, follow the steps below.

You will need: (this recipe serves 4)

1 ripe pomegranate • a large container of plain yogurt (32 oz) • 9 shortbread cookies • some fresh mint leaves

1. Place eight of your shortbread cookies in a plastic food bag. Carefully use the end of a rolling pin to bash them into small pieces.

2. Remove the cookie crumbs from the plastic bag and divide them between four glasses.

3. Carefully cut the pomegranate into quarters and place in a large bowl of water.

4. Keeping the pomegranate below the surface of the water, use your fingers to remove all the seeds. The seeds will sink to the bottom and any white pith will float to the top.

5. Remove the pith from the top of the water with your hands, then use a strainer to drain the seeds.

6. Empty the yogurt into a mixing bowl and add the pomegranate seeds. Use a metal spoon to mix them together, and watch as the yogurt turns pink.

7. Spoon the pink yogurt mixture into each of the glasses.

8. Crumble some of the extra shortbread cookie on top of the pudding and decorate with a few fresh mint leaves. Serve with a spoon. Yum!

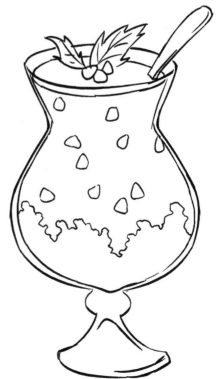

SECRET SAFARI

You're visiting a safari park, but where are all the animals?

Below is a map of the safari park. To read it, you will need to use coordinates. A coordinate is a letter and a number that refers to a location on a map. To use a coordinate, place your finger on the letter on the left-hand side of the map. Trace your finger along the row to the column that matches the number. In that square you will find the animal that the coordinate refers to.

Can you figure out which animals live at the following coordinates?
Check your answers on page 93.

I. D3 **2.** BI **3.** F3 **4.** C6 **5.** A4 **6.** E6

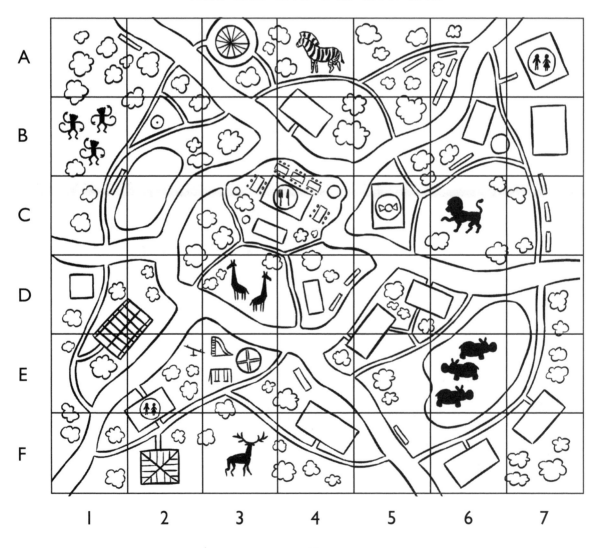

WHAT'S YOUR SUMMER STYLE?

Answer A, B, C, or D to the questions below, then find out which summer style fits you best on the next page.

1. Your friend turns up at your house unexpectedly. What are you wearing?

A. Sweatpants and sneakers

B. A spa-style bathrobe

C. A new dress

D. A pair of designer jeans

2. What is your favorite way to spend a summer afternoon?

A. Playing Frisbee in the park

B. Relaxing on a deck chair

C. Going for a picnic with a friend

D. Working on a craft project

3. What is your favorite summer breakfast?

A. Scrambled eggs and orange juice

B. Yogurt with fruit and honey

C. Croissants with butter and jam

D. Homemade granola

4. Which of the following best describes your ideal perfume?

A. Fresh and fruity

B. Deep and musky

C. The newest one in the store

D. A mixture of your favorite essential oils

5. What kind of bag do you pack for a sleepover?

A. A gym bag

B. An oversize beach bag

C. A small, stylish suitcase

D. The bag you sewed together last weekend

6. What is your summer hairstyle?

A. A ponytail

B. A glamorous blowout

C. You like to change your hairstyle regularly

D. Accessorized hairstyle with lots of clips, hair bands, etc.

WHAT YOUR ANSWERS MEAN

Count up how many of each letter you have chosen. Now look below to find out what your answers say about your style. If you scored an even mix of letters, this means you have a totally unique summer style—you go, girl!

MOSTLY As:
SPORTS SUPERSTAR

You're an active girl who's always bursting with energy. You like to spend time outside and love meeting up with your friends to play team games. You're superfit and always have a healthy glow. Why not turn to pages 12 and 13 to find out how to make up your own dance routine?

MOSTLY Cs:
FASHIONABLE FRIEND

You love flicking through fashion magazines, and your friends look to you as someone who is always ahead of the latest trends. Turn to pages 56 and 57 to learn how to hold a Summer Swap Shop.

MOSTLY Bs:
GORGEOUS GODDESS

For you, summer vacation is about taking time out to pamper yourself. Your bedroom could compete with any of the top spas. You feel comfortable in any clothes—as long as your hair and skin are looking good, you don't care! Turn to pages 8 and 9 for some summery beauty tips.

MOSTLY Ds:
CREATIVE KITTEN

You're an artsy girl who likes to dress differently from your friends. You're great at making the latest fashions your own and use your summer vacation to put your ideas into practice. Turn to pages 80 and 81 for a creative project that will last you all summer.

WACKY WINDOW BOOTS

Brighten up your windowsill with these wacky rain-boot flower pots!

You will need:

acrylic paints (or a selection of nail polishes in different shades will do) • paintbrushes • a pair of old rain boots • a metal corkscrew • some soil and gravel • a selection of seeds or plants

1. Paint a design of your choice directly onto both boots. (Always rinse out your brushes with water when you have finished painting.)

2. Ask an adult to carefully pierce a small hole through the sole of each boot using a corkscrew. This hole allows excess water to drain out of your boots.

3. Pour a cup of gravel into each boot and then fill the boot up to the top with soil.

4. Bury some seeds just under the surface of the soil and pour some water over them. Place the boots on a small plate to catch any excess water, then place them on a sunny windowsill.

5. Water your boots once a week, or if it's really hot, every other day.

WHAT SHALL YOUR GARDEN GROW?

Here are some ideas to get you started:

• Herbs and edible plants: parsley, basil, or mint
• Pretty flowers: sunflowers, marigolds, or pansies
• Fragrant flowers: lavender or sweet pea.

Tip: Plant ready-grown flowers rather than seeds for instantly pretty pots.

43

MOVIE THEATER RACERS

It's Friday afternoon and you're meeting your friends for a movie. Race your friends through the park to get there before the show is sold out!

Place a coin for each player in the start box, then take turns spinning the spinner (follow the instructions opposite to find out how) and moving forward the number of spaces shown.

School

Movies

Take a shortcut through the park. Jump ahead.

You drop your wallet. Move back three spaces to look for it.

The new sneakers you put on this morning help you run faster. Move forward three spaces.

MOVIES

FINISH

You get stuck in line. Lose a turn.

You see your brother and he lends you his skateboard. Take another turn.

SCHOOL

SPINNER

1 2 3 4 5 6

Cut out this spinner and pierce a toothpick through the center.

To spin your spinner, hold the toothpick on your playing surface and spin it between your thumb and forefinger. When it stops spinning, the number at the top of the spinner is the number of spaces you should move your coin.

START

You left your bag at school and had to go back and get it. Lose a turn.

There's a kitten stuck in a tree. Lose a turn while you get it down.

Use the bridge to cross over the park lake. Jump ahead.

You see a cute puppy and stop to say hello. Lose a turn.

The sun is shining on you! Spin again to take another turn.

BACK OF SPINNER

Fill the page with flowers, butterflies, bees, and ladybugs.

MIND GAMES

These fun games trick the brain and the body.

SAY WHEN

Ask a friend to hold out her arm and close her eyes. Start stroking the inside of her arm just above her wrist, moving up, down, and sideways, but gradually heading toward the inside of her elbow. Tell her to shout when she thinks your finger is directly on the dip at the inside of her elbow. You'd be surprised how many people get this wrong.

BILLY GOAT GRUFF

Ask a friend to stand or sit with her back to you. Say "How many horns does the billy goat have?" At the same time, press some of the fingers of one hand into her back—spread them as wide as you can. Your friend has to guess how many fingers you are using. The best thing about this game is that young people tend to be better at guessing than adults.

THROUGH THE FLOOR

Ask a friend to lie on her back on the floor. Grab her ankles and lift her feet off the floor until they're level with your waist.

Ask her to shut her eyes and breathe deeply. Hold her legs in this position for one minute, then very slowly lower them toward the ground. Your friend will expect her legs to reach the floor long before they actually do. She will feel as if her legs are passing through the floor!

Draw your dream vacation destination.

BORED ON BOARD?

Try out these games and time will fly.

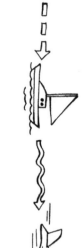

IN MY SUITCASE I HAVE PACKED . . .

The first player says, "In my suitcase I have packed . . ." then names an item beginning with A, such as "an alarm clock."

The second player then says, "In my suitcase I have packed . . . ," and then says the previous item, and one of their own that begins with a B, for example, "an alarm clock and a ball."

The game continues until you have been through the whole alphabet or until a player forgets one of the items.

CELEBRITY INTERVIEW

Take turns pretending to be a famous person who is being interviewed for a radio show. The other players must ask you questions and use your answers to guess who you are.

COLORFUL CARS

Each player picks a color. The winner is the first to see thirty cars of their chosen color.

ODD OR EVEN

Each player chooses "odd" or "even." On the count of three, all players raise their hands, each holding up as many fingers as they want.

Count up the total number of fingers raised to find out if it is an odd or an even number. Those who guessed correctly score a point.

FAMILY ACT

Take turns acting like one of your family members. The first person to guess who you are pretending to be scores a point and gets to go next.

Note: Make sure no one gets offended—these games are supposed to make your summer more fun, not more stressful!

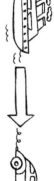

BEACH BEAUTY

You're armed with your towel, shades, sunscreen, and snorkel. You're ready to have a splashing time at the seaside, but a girl has her image to think of. Follow these handy hints to be a beautiful beach babe.

SUMMER HAIR

Fun on the beach can be a nightmare for your hair—the sun and seawater will dry it out.

Keep your locks feeling silky and fight the frizz by slicking lots of leave-in conditioner onto your hair and combing it through. If your hair is long enough, pull it into a ponytail for extra protection.

Everyone knows sunscreen is essential for anyone venturing out in the sun, but there's nothing worse than a red, sunburned hair part. Always keep the top of your head protected with a hat. Alternatively, tie a head scarf, with the ends behind your head, for a superstylish cover-up.

SURFER STYLE

Surfer girls' hair always looks beautifully messy, "tousled" by fun in the sun, sea, and sand.

If you don't get to the beach, you can get the surfer-girl-hair look by mixing two tablespoons of salt in two cups of warm water. Pour it over your hair after shampooing and don't rinse it out. This salty rinse will give your hair a cool beach-babe look.

WORKING THE WAVES

If it is long enough, wear your hair in braids all day at the beach. In the evening, brush your hair loose for soft, glamorous waves.

SUMMER FEET

Summer is the time to be bold, so paint your toenails with some bright polish.

Why not try painting each nail a different shade? Or, for a truly eye-catching look, use a dark color first and then add a stripe of a different color down the middle of each nail.

For supersoft summer feet, put lots of moisturizer all over your feet before bedtime. Put on a pair of old socks to protect your sheets. This helps to keep moisture locked into the skin of your feet, making them extra soft.

Getting sand between your toes can be annoying, but walking barefoot on the beach rubs away dead skin, leaving the soles of your feet feeling lovely and smooth.

SAND CASTLE SURPRISE

Everyone wants to be queen of the castle, but this page will make sure it's you who wears the crown, with the best sand castle on the beach.

1. The perfect spot. Choose a site close enough to the sea that you can easily get water, but not so close that your masterpiece will get washed away. Look for the point where the dark, wet sand starts to turn lighter.

2. Prepare the area. Pour buckets of water onto your chosen area and stomp down the sand until you have a firm area large enough for your sand castle.

3. Build a base. Build up a large mound of wet sand with a flat top. Pat down the sand as you build up the mound to create a firm, flat base for your sand castle.

4. Make the castle. Did you know that there's a scientific formula for building the perfect sand castle? Scientists have discovered that the winning recipe is found when you mix one bucket of

Complete this sand castle.

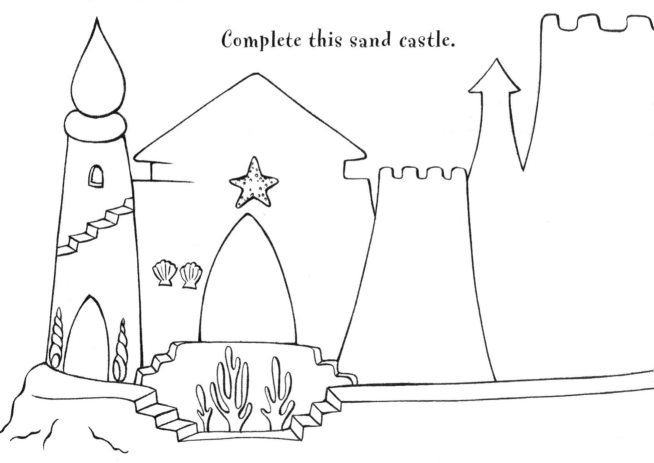

water with eight buckets of sand to create the perfect sand mixture. Fill your buckets with the mixture, pat the sand down with your shovel so that it's flat and compact, then carefully tip over the buckets on top of the mound. One large castle in the middle with four smaller "turret" sand castles around it looks particularly impressive.

5. Make a moat and castle wall. A moat is a deep trench filled with water that's built around a castle to protect it from attack. Dig out the sand at the base of your sand castle mound to create a trench that goes all the way around it. Use the sand you've dug out to build up a wall around the outside of the trench. The wall should be about as tall as your hand and as wide as your wrist.

6. Fill the moat with water. Create a trench that goes from the sea to your moat. Start by creating a passageway through the castle wall for the water to pass through. To do this, use your finger to carefully cut an arch into the area of the wall facing the sea. Next, dig a deep trench all the way from the archway to the sea. The seawater will rush down the trench toward your sand castle and fill the moat, guarding it from invaders and protecting your castle.

TREASURE ISLAND

Ahoy there! Head to the treasure island for some puzzle and doodle fun.

A girl is on an island with her mean brother and greedy sister and a bag of candy. She needs to get herself, her brother, and her sister back to the mainland with the candy. The raft she has is only large enough to carry her and one thing she needs to take with her, so she will need to make several trips.

The problem is, she can't leave her brother alone with her sister because he will tease her. She can't leave her sister alone with the candy, or else she will eat it all. Her brother will not eat the candy, so he can be left alone with it.

Can you figure out what she can do? Answer is on page 93.

What would you take to a desert island?

BEACH SUDOKU

Complete the grid so that each column, each row, and each of the four larger squares contains only one bucket, a shovel, a sand castle, and an ice-cream cone.

Answer is on page 93.

Fill the chest with treasure.

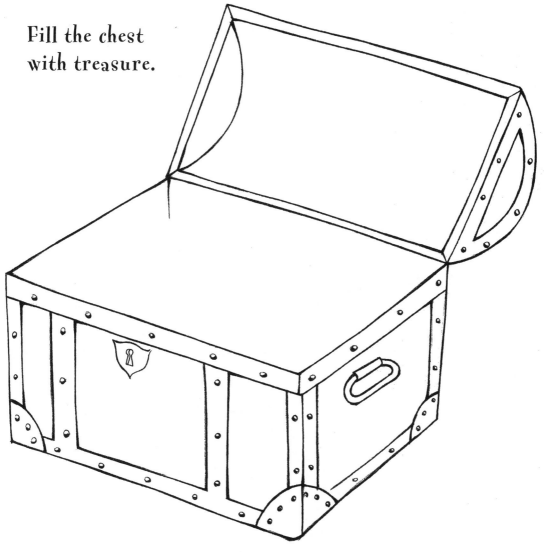

CLOTHING SWAP

If you're bored with your clothes and have a closet full of items that you don't wear anymore, why not host a Summer Swap Shop? Follow the steps below and see what sassy new style you end up with.

1. Choose a date for your Summer Swap Shop and invite your friends to your house.

2. Ask each friend to bring any clothes, shoes, or accessories that they don't wear anymore and would be happy to swap for something new.

3. On the day of the clothing swap, designate areas of a room for different items—these might include skirts, tops, dresses, hats, belts, scarves, etc.

4. Cut out a different colored square of paper for each of the designated areas. Stick a colored square on the floor, table, or chair next to each area.

5. As your guests arrive, ask them to place their items of clothing in the correct areas.

6. Write the name of each guest on a different colored square of paper—one for each item of clothing that they brought to the shop. For example, if skirts are in the red area, write the guest's name that brought a skirt on a red square.

7. Put all of the squares with names on them into a large bowl and mix them up. Take turns pulling a ticket out of the bowl. The guest named on the ticket can then choose an item of clothing from the appropriately colored pile.

PLAY THE "STEAL THAT STYLE" GAME

Read on for a different swapping game called "Steal That Style." This is a fun game to play at a clothing swap—the aim is to decide who gets to keep what.

1. Put all the clothes in the middle of the floor.

2. Each player must then choose one of the styles listed below or think of one of her own.

Boho-Chic   **Main Street Cool**   **Sari Sensation**

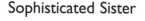

Beach Babe   **Sophisticated Sister**   **Emo**

3. Two players then have one minute to look through all the clothes and accessories on display and put together an outfit in their chosen style.

4. The two players then model their outfits. Why not clear a catwalk down the center of the room for them to walk down like models?

5. The other players then vote for which of the models has done the best job of recreating the style. The model who wins gets to keep one item from her outfit.

6. Repeat with other players and other styles. Happy swapping!

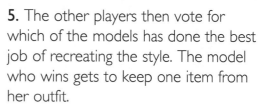

FASHION FRENZY

Backstage at a fashion show, things aren't going well.
Can you solve the problems and help the show run smoothly?
Check your answers on page 94.

MODEL MATCH

These models are supposed to be walking down the catwalk with dogs in their handbags, but their bags have all been mixed up. Follow the leashes to find out which bag belongs to which model.

SHOE SEARCH

These models are due on the catwalk in three minutes—can you help them find their missing shoes to complete the matching pairs? Which poor model doesn't have a matching pair?

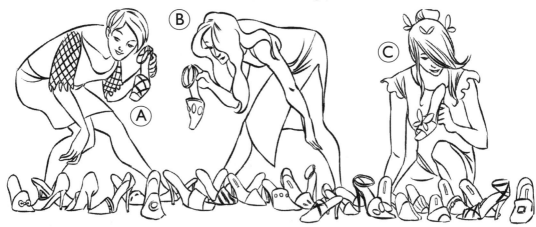

MAKEUP MAYHEM

The makeup artist has just thrown a tantrum and quit! Quick: Use colored pencils to give these models makeovers that match the theme of their shows.

Hollywood Glamour

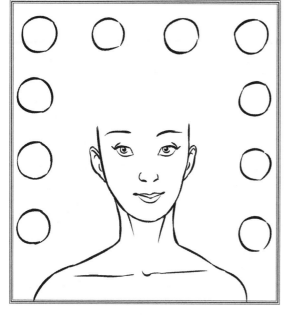

'80s Retro

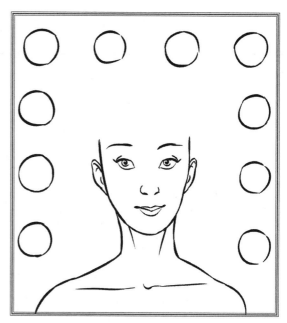

Vampire Chic

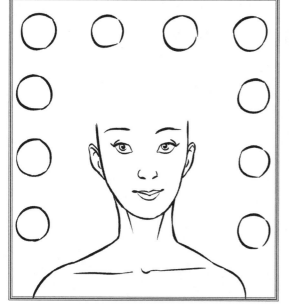

Natural Beauty

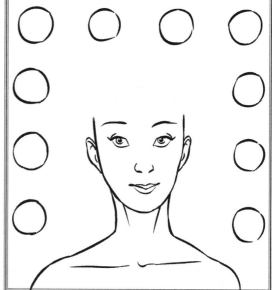

ALL THE FUN OF THE FAIR

Step right up! Turn your living room into an amusement park
with these fun games, then invite your friends to come and play.

ROLL UP FOR THE RAFFLE

1. Find three items that you don't mind giving up
as prizes for your raffle, such as a teddy bear, a
chocolate bar, and a funky headband.

2. Write the numbers 103, 107, and 115 on a
piece of paper and cut them out. Use tape to stick
them to your prizes.

3. Fold a piece of 8½ x 11 paper in half four times,
then unfold it so that you can see the rectangular
fold lines. Starting at one hundred, write a number
in each of the rectangles, as shown, until you reach
one hundred fifteen. Cut along the fold lines and
fold each rectangle in half. Place all the folded
pieces of paper into a bowl.

100	101	102	103
104	105	106	107
108	109	110	111
112	113	114	115

4. To enter the raffle, each player must choose a piece of paper from the bowl. If the
number matches one of the numbers stuck to a prize, the player wins that prize.

BEST ANIMAL IN SHOW

Ask your guests to bring their best stuffed animal to the fair and explain why
theirs is the best, including any special tricks they can perform. Each guest has
to give each animal marks out of ten for appearance, special features, and
lovability. Whichever animal has scored the most points wins "best in show."

SPLAT THE RAT!

1. Make a "rat" by cutting the feet off an old pair of tights and stuffing one foot inside the other. Tie it at the top with string. Use felt-tip pens to draw eyes, a nose, and whiskers onto the stuffed part.

Make sure your rat is small enough to easily slide through a cardboard tube from inside a roll of wrapping paper.

2. Use tape to attach the cardboard tube to a large piece of poster board.

3. Use felt-tip pens to write "Splat the Rat" onto the card, then use a removable adhesive to attach the card to the wall. The bottom of the tube should be just below your knee.

4. Each player must be given a paper towel roll tube to use as a bat. Drop the rat through the long tube for the player to try to hit the rat with the bat before it reaches the floor.

BOWLING SOCK BALLS

1. Line up a collection of seven clean, empty yogurt containers upside down on the floor. Write a number from one to seven on a piece of paper and cut out each number. Place a number randomly under each yogurt container.

2. Place a piece of 8½ x 11 paper on the floor about six feet away from the containers. Roll up a pair of socks into a ball.

3. Players must then take turns rolling the sock ball across the floor from the piece of paper to knock over as many yogurt containers as possible. Count up the points from inside each yogurt container the player knocked over and write down their score. The person with the most points is the winner.

CAMPFIRE TWISTS

It's time to get cooking by the campfire!

These delicious treats are perfect to bake over a campfire. You don't need to measure out the ingredients, and you don't even need any cooking utensils.

1. Make a pile of flour and scoop out the center to form a well.

2. Pour a little water into the well and mix together with your hands until you have a lump of dough. Don't worry if it gets messy. Add more flour or water if you need to.

3. Shape the dough with your hands into a large square.

4. Sprinkle lots of chocolate chips onto the middle of the dough, then fold it so that all the chocolate chips are on the inside.

5. Roll out the dough into a long sausage shape.

6. Twist the dough around a skewer or stick and toast over the glowing embers of your campfire.

PHOTO FRENZY

Can you figure out which parent took each of the photos below?

You need to think about where each parent is standing and which girl they are aiming their camera at. You'll find the answers on page 94.

SHOP 'TIL YOU DROP

Complete the puzzles and turn to page 94 to check your answers.

You have $3.00 in your purse. If you were going to use all of your money to buy one type of candy, how many of each type could you buy?

Can you find the sunglasses below that match the ones pictured in the magazine above?

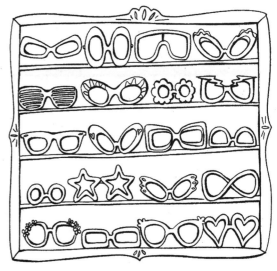

Can you find eleven differences between the two window displays on the opposite page?

TRAVEL BINGO

This is a great game that you can play anywhere—on a long car ride, on a rainy day, or even at the beach.

Travel Bingo is a game for three players. Find out how to play below, then cut out the boards and counters on the next page, and you're ready for some bingo fun.

1. You are all going on vacation together, but one player has lost her suitcase and needs to borrow items from the other two. Choose which of you will be the "suitcase" players and who will be the "lost luggage" player.

2. Cut out the suitcase game boards and each of the counters. The two "suitcase" players then choose either the suitcase and counters with the hearts or the ones with the flowers. (See page 68.)

3. Without letting the "lost luggage" player see, the two "suitcase" players choose six of their counters and place

them all faceup on their suitcase game boards.

4. The "lost luggage" player then calls out in a random order the items from the list below that they would like to borrow.

5. Each time the "lost luggage" player says the name of an item that one of the "suitcase" players has on their game board, that player hands the matching counter to the "lost luggage" player. The winner is the first player to hand over all the items that are on her suitcase game board.

LIST OF ITEMS

1. Candy	7. Sunglasses
2. T-shirt	8. Magazine
3. Towel	9. Purse
4. Camera	10. Money
5. Toothpaste	11. Hat
6. Hairbrush	12. Neck pillow

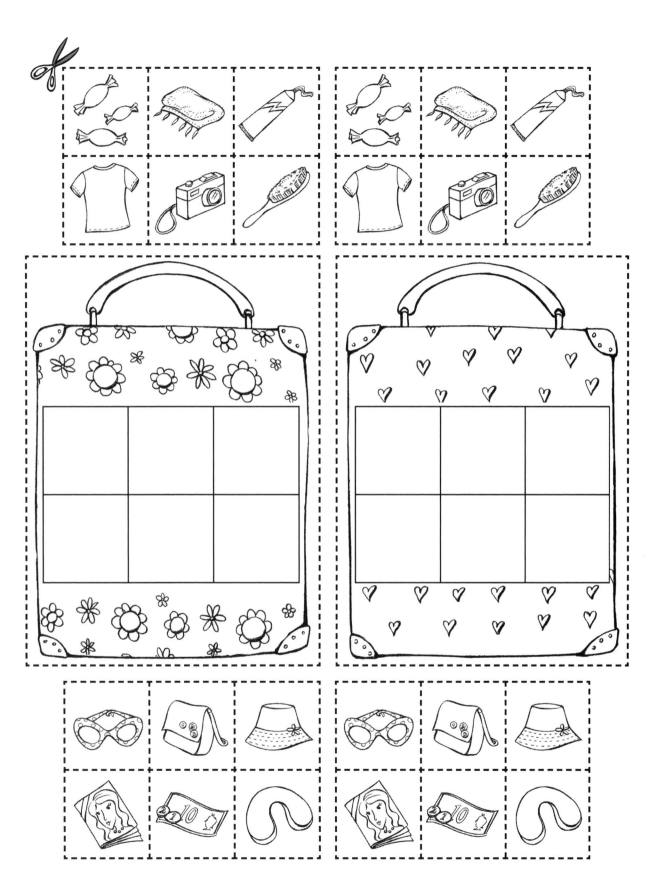

BAGS OF DIFFERENCE

Oh no! Your bag has been mixed up with someone else's at the airport.
Can you find five differences between your bag (A) and the other bag?
Answers are on page 94.

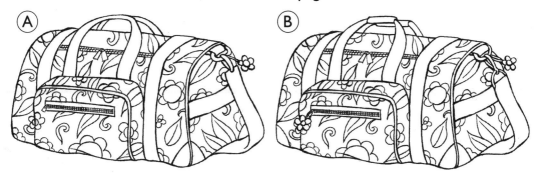

What have you packed in your suitcase?

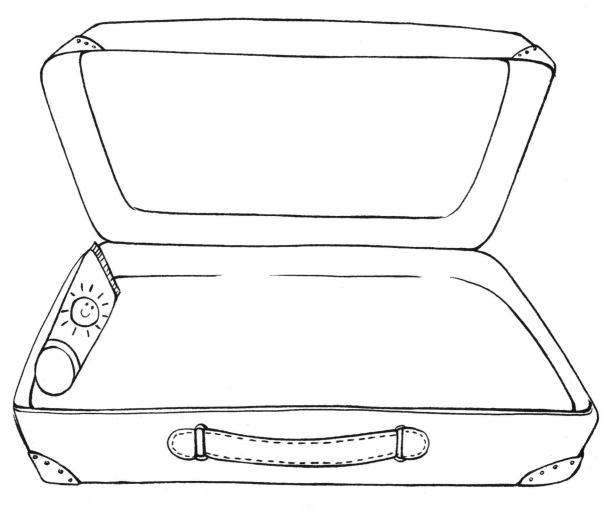

SUMMER BY THE SEA

Complete these seaside-themed puzzles and turn to page 95
to check your answers.

Which four of the details below are from the picture of the tide pool?

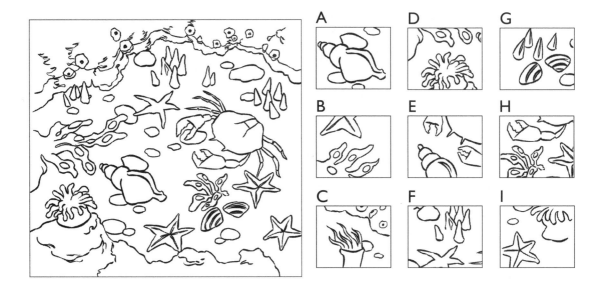

Which two of these ice-cream sundaes are identical?

Look at these beach volleyball players.

A. How many of the players are wearing shorts?

B. How many have at least one arm in the air?

C. How many are wearing flip-flops?

D. How many are wearing sunglasses?

Design the sails on these boats.

GO GREEN

Saving energy over summer vacation will help save the planet.

Read the facts below to find out how to go green this summer, then follow the
doodle instructions to make the house planet-friendly.

GREEN GUIDES

- Ask an adult to unplug electrical appliances when you leave home to save
  energy. Never leave them on standby (with a red light shining), as this uses   up
  energy.

- Find out where the local bike-rental shop is and get cycling. Riding a bike is
  much better for the environment than using a car.

- Go green at the supermarket by encouraging your parents to only buy locally
  grown fruits and vegetables—not items that have been flown in from around
  the world. When you get home, why not grow your own fruits and vegetables
  in your garden or in a window box?

Fill the vegetable
patch with
home-grown
vegetables.

Give her bike
wheels so
it's ready to ride.

- Save water by turning the taps off while you brush your teeth.

- Recycling bottles, cans, paper, and cardboard will mean your garbage gets turned into something else, which saves energy. Ask at the local information office to find out where the recycling bins are located.

Draw the TV. Make sure it is turned off.

Draw the curtains to let natural light in and save electricity.

Fill the washing machine with your laundry.

Fill the recycling bin with bottles, paper, and cans.

FUN ON THE FARM

There's lots going on down on the farm in the summertime. Complete these farmyard puzzles, then check your answers on page 95.

How many birds and how many apples can you find in the orchard?

Can you find five differences between the two horses with their foals?

Can you help the dog find his way home through the woods?

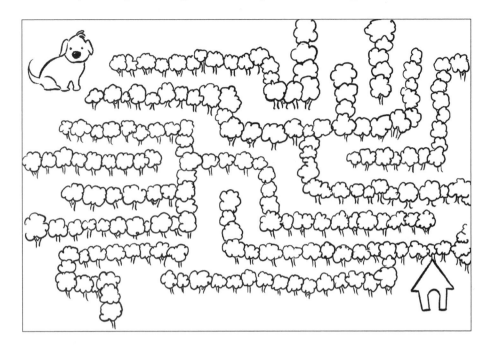

These cows are jealous of their stylish friend. Give them similar spotty patterns.

SUMMER SPINNERS

Liven up your garden or window box with these
special pinwheels.

You will need:

3 pieces of plain paper • a thumbtack
• a pencil with an eraser on the end • scissors • a glue stick • felt-tip pens

I. Trace the pattern below onto two pieces of paper, but only write the letters on one of the pieces of paper.

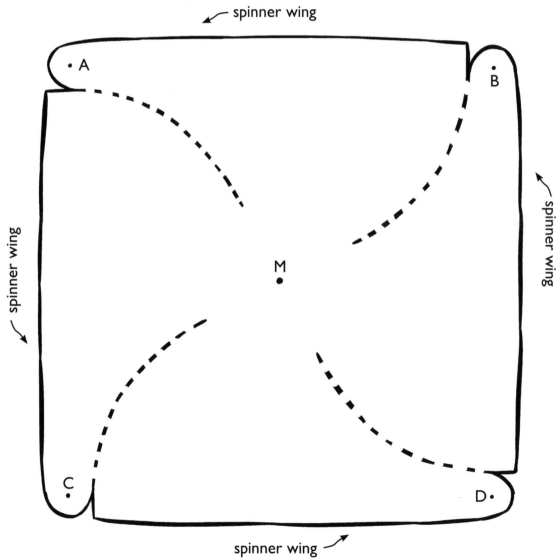

spinner wing

spinner wing

spinner wing

spinner wing

A

B

C

D

M

2. Carefully cut out each pattern along the solid lines.

3. Line up the two shapes so that they fit nicely back-to-back. Glue them together.

4. Using your felt-tip pens, doodle a different design on each side of the spinner shape—why not draw flowers and spots on one side and cherries and stripes on the other?

5. Trace the star shape below onto the third piece of paper.

Draw a dot in the middle of the star. Color in the star shape and cut it out.

6. Carefully cut along the four dotted lines of the spinner shape.

7. Fold the corners of the spinner wings (the areas labeled A, B, C, and D) into the middle of the spinner shape (M).

8. Use the thumbtack to carefully poke a hole through the dot in the center of the star. Now pierce a hole through each of the spinner wings—each wing should now be pinned behind the star.

9. Carefully push the end of the pin into the side of the eraser on the end of the pencil.

10. Place on your windowsill or in your garden on a breezy summer's day, and watch it spin and make pretty patterns.

Decorate these summer spinners.

GARDEN GAMES

The girls are having plenty of fun in the sun in the garden scene below.
Why not join in the fun by completing these puzzles?
Answers are on page 95.

Using only three straight lines, divide the garden scene below so that there
are only two girls in each section.

Can you find the following animals and insects in the garden scene above?

eleven birds • seven butterflies • five cats • seven ladybugs • three mice

Fill the page with summer fruits.

SEW... FANTASTIC!

Summer vacation is the perfect time to get creative.

Add color and texture to your bedroom with a range of throw pillows made from different fabrics. Here's how to make your own. (You may want to ask an adult for help.)

For each pillow you will need:

an old pillow • a length of fabric (big enough to wrap around the pillow)
• thread in a color that matches your fabric • a needle • scissors • sewing pins
• beads, buttons, and so on to decorate • old newspaper • 2 lengths of ribbon

1. Carefully cut out a piece of fabric that is roughly twice the size of the pillow, leaving an extra 2 inches of width around the edges.

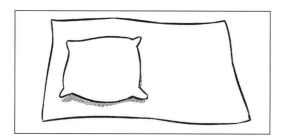

2. Fold the fabric in half, as shown below.

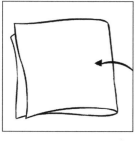

3. Place sewing pins along the outside edges of the fabric to hold it together. Leave one side of your square unpinned.

4. Thread your needle using roughly 5 feet of thread. Tie a double knot in the end of it. Push the needle through one corner, closest to the fold of the pillowcase. Pull through on the other side of the knot.

5. Pull the needle back through the fabric about ½ inch ahead of your original point and again, gently pull the thread through.

Once you have done this, push the needle back through the fabric in the same point that you started. Pull the thread through. Now push the needle through the fabric again, roughly ¼ inch ahead of the last point, as shown below. Note: Remove the sewing pins as you sew past them.

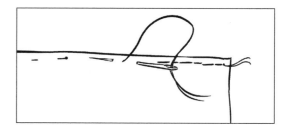

6. Continue sewing in this way in a straight line until you are about ½ inch from the next corner.

7. Rotate the fabric a quarter turn and sew along the next edge as you did in step **5**.

8. When you reach the next corner of the pillowcase, secure your stitches by sewing over the same spot ten times. Carefully cut off any excess thread.

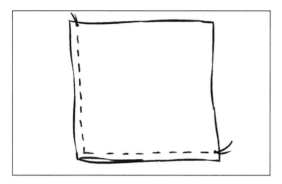

9. Turn the pillowcase right side out and place a piece of newspaper inside it—this will stop you sewing through both sides of the fabric in the next step.

10. Decorate one side of the cushion cover by stitching on buttons, beads, sequins, and colored feathers to create your own design. Remove the newspaper when you are done.

11. Insert the old pillow inside the new case along the open end.

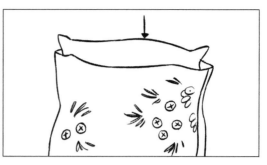

12. Carefully use the scissors to make two snips in the top layer of fabric. The snips should divide the open end into thirds, and be about 1 inch from the edge of the fabric. Make identical snips in the same places on the bottom layer of fabric.

13. Use the lengths of ribbon to close the pillowcase by tying the top layer of fabric to the bottom layer. Secure with a bow.

14. Make as many throw pillows as you want and scatter them over your bed or give them as presents to your friends and family.

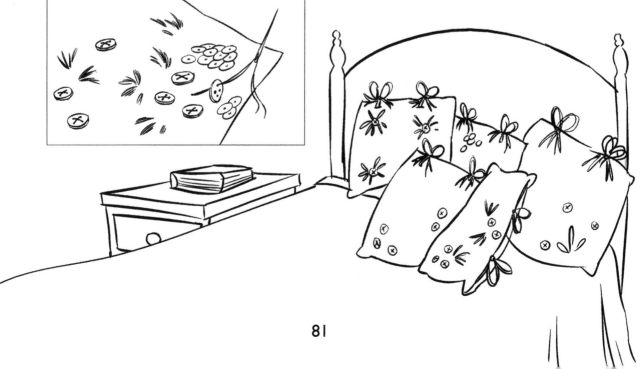

STAY COOL

When the temperature rises, keep your cool with these hot tips.

HOTHEAD

If your head's cool, the rest of your body will be, too. To cool down, simply dip a head scarf in cold water, then wring it out so that it's damp, but not dripping. Wrap it over your head and tie it in a pretty bow at the base of your neck.

WATERMELONADE

This delicious watermelon lemonade is perfect for cooling yourself down on a hot day. Cut slices of watermelon, remove the peel, and pick out the seeds. Blend in a food processor—ask an adult to help you with this.

Press the pulped watermelon through a strainer into a large jug. Add lemonade and mix together with a whisk. Garnish with slices of watermelon and a sprig of mint.

FRUITY CUBES

Fill an ice cube tray with water. Cut pieces of lemon and lime and place one in each cube. Carefully slide the tray into your freezer and leave for a couple of hours. Add to summer drinks for a cool, citrus chill.

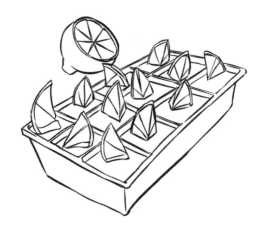

OCEAN SPRAY

Find an empty bottle with a spray function—hair products and suntan lotions often come in this kind of bottle. Thoroughly wash the bottle so that there's none of the old product left inside.

Fill the bottle with water and squirt a little of your favorite perfume into the bottle. Keep it in the fridge and use it to have a quick, refreshing spray after being outdoors.

FAN-TASTIC

Draw a pretty pattern on a piece of 8½ × 11 paper. Pleat the paper by folding every inch, as shown below.

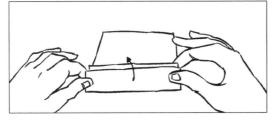

Take two Popsicle sticks and glue one to each end of the paper so that the top of each stick is in line with the top of the paper. Tie a piece of ribbon around the bottom of the paper to create a handle.

WATER COOLER

Keep bottles of drinking water in the freezer and take one with you when you're going out to play in the sunshine. The ice will gradually melt, giving you a supply of cool, refreshing water.

If you are hot when you go to bed at night, place a bottle of frozen water in front of a fan. The chilled air will get pushed around the room and cool you down.

SUMMER MAGIC

Add a bit of magic to your summer with these clever tricks!

HOW TO SAW A LADY IN HALF

Fool your friends into thinking you are cutting a lady in half. Luckily she is made of paper, so if anything does go wrong, no one gets hurt!

You will need:

paper • pen • envelope • scissors

1. To prepare this trick, first seal the envelope shut, then carefully cut off the ends to create a tube shape.

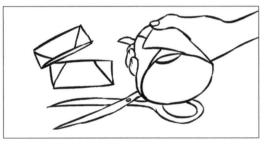

2. Flatten out the tube again so that the top and bottom of the envelope meet in the middle. Carefully cut two slits from the new edge up to just before the central crease. The slits should separate the tube into thirds.

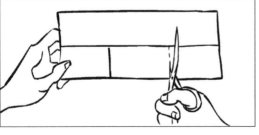

3. Cut a strip of paper roughly 4 inches wide and about 2 inches longer than the length of your flattened tube shape.

4. Draw a picture of a lady onto the piece of paper, like this:

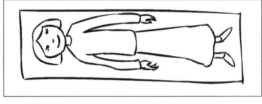

5. Reshape the flattened tube so that it forms a tube shape again. Position it in the palm of your hand so that the slits are at the back.

6. Slide the paper lady (picture side facing upward) inside the tube shape, pushing her feet through the first slit so that they come out of the back of the envelope, and then bring her feet back inside the tube by pushing them through the second slit. The back of the tube shape should now look like this:

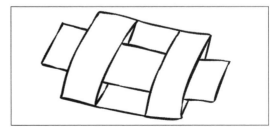

7. To perform the trick, cut the tube in half, making sure that your scissors cut through the middle of the tube—being careful to cut above the paper lady.

8. Finally, pull the lady out from the two pieces of envelope, and amaze your audience when she appears unharmed!

HOW TO CHANGE A BALLOON'S COLOR

Learn how to make a balloon magically change color . . . just by popping it!

You will need:

a green balloon • a yellow balloon • adhesive tape • a pencil • a pin

1. Before performing this trick, you will need to first make a double-sided loop of tape. Stick it onto the middle of the yellow balloon.

2. Push the unsharpened end of a pencil into the yellow balloon's neck. Then, push the same end into the green balloon. Slide it down until it is completely inside the green balloon.

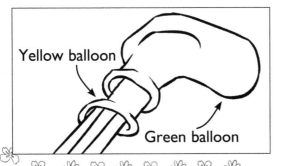

Yellow balloon

Green balloon

3. Blow up the yellow balloon (which will also blow up the green balloon outside it) and tie a knot in the bottom of both balloon necks.

4. Now stand in front of your audience, holding what they will think is a blown-up green balloon.

5. Locate where the tape is on the yellow balloon by looking through the green balloon on the outside. Jab a pin in here.

The green balloon will burst, revealing the yellow balloon inside it. It will look like the balloon has magically changed color!

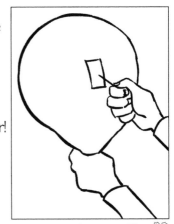

HOME SWEET HOME

Summer vacation is perfect for enjoying time at home. So relax and settle down to these homey puzzles. All the answers are on pages 95 and 96.

SUDO-COOK

Complete this sudoku grid so that the four different kitchen items shown below—the oven mitt, the spoon, the saucepan, and the mixing bowl—appear only once in each column, each row, and in each of the four larger squares.

TEACUP MIX-UP

Can you match the teacups to their saucers below?

BUNK BED MADNESS

Four sleepy girls want to go to bed. Can you find which bunk belongs to which girl?

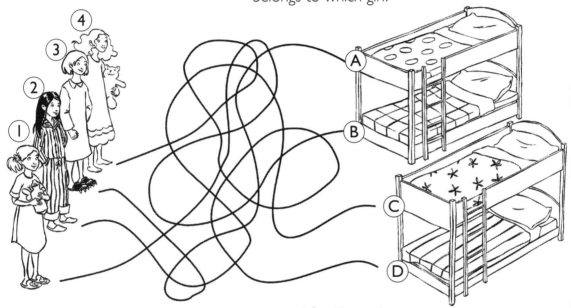

DREAM WORLD

You dream you are lost in a strange house. Can you find your way through the maze of corridors to your bedroom?

SUMMER HIGHLIGHTS

You'll want to remember your summer forever, so answer these questions at the end of it to keep a record of the highlights.

Dates: From: .... To: ....

Who did you hang out with?

What was the funniest thing that happened?

Describe where you spent the summer.

If you could relive one day of your summer, which would it be?

What was your favorite outdoor activity?

What was the most delicious thing you ate?

Was there anything that you did for the first time during your summer?

What was your favorite summer outfit?

Did you make any new friends? What are they like?

What will you miss most now that you're heading back to school?

Fill these picture frames with your favorite summer memories.

ALL THE ANSWERS

SUMMER SNAPS
page 5

1. E   3. A   5. F
2. D   4. B   6. C

PICNIC PUZZLE
page 19

[11] Strawberries
(6) Cupcakes

TRAVEL TRIVIA
pages 20 and 21

1. C   4. C   7. D   10. A
2. B   5. C   8. B   11. C
3. B   6. A   9. A   12. B

SURFER GIRLS
page 23

A. five   **B.** seven   **C.** two   **D.** seven

CRACK THOSE CODES
page 27

Bottle 1 used clue 2:
Riddle: "I have arms, legs, and a back, but I never walk anywhere. What am I?"
Answer: I am a chair.

Bottle 2 used clue 3:
Riddle: "Say it and you will break it. What is it?"
Answer: Silence.

Bottle 3 used clue 1:
Riddle: "The more you take of these, the more you leave behind. What are they?"
Answer: Footsteps.

WATER WORLD
pages 34 and 35

Swimmer A reaches chute 1.
Swimmer B reaches chute 2.
Swimmer C reaches chute 3.
Swimmer D reaches chute 4.

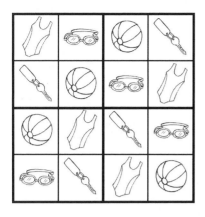

FIND THE FASHIONISTAS
page 37

The matching girls are *E* and *H*.

SECRET SAFARI
page 40

1. Giraffes
2. Monkeys
3. Deer
4. Lion
5. Zebra
6. Hippos

TREASURE ISLAND
page 54

The girl takes her sister across to the mainland, leaving her brother and the candy. She returns to the island and takes her brother to the mainland. Then she takes her sister back to the island with her—so that her brother and sister aren't left alone together.

Next, she leaves her sister on the island, takes the candy across to the mainland, and leaves it with her brother. Finally, she returns to the island and takes her sister back to the mainland.

BEACH SUDOKU
page 55

FASHION FRENZY
page 58

Model *A* has dog 5.
Model *B* has dog 4.
Model *C* has dog 2.
Model *D* has dog 1.
Model *E* has dog 3.

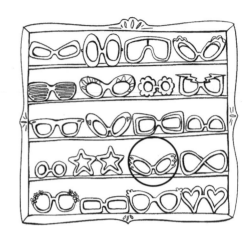

Model *C* doesn't have a matching pair.

PHOTO FRENZY
page 63

A. 2 **C.** 5 **E.** 3
B. 4 **D.** 1 **F.** 6

SHOP 'TIL YOU DROP
pages 64 and 65

In the candy shop you could buy:
17 cola bottles with 11¢ left over,
6 bonbons, 30 mints, 15 taffies,
9 lollipops with 3¢ left over,
5 licorices, 3 candy canes with 45¢ left
over, 12 gummy mice, or
6 lemon drops with 30¢ left over

BAGS OF DIFFERENCE
page 69

B

SUMMER BY THE SEA
pages 70 and 71

Squares *A*, *D*, *F*, and *H*.

A. Six   **C**. Seven
B. Five   **D**. Zero

FUN ON THE FARM
pages 74 and 75

 apples    birds

GARDEN GAMES
page 78

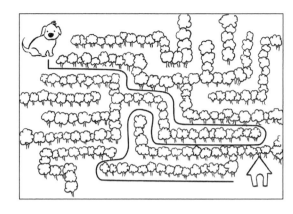

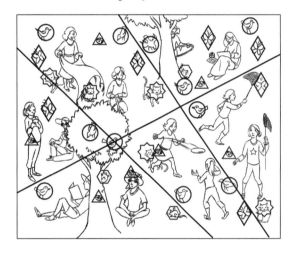

HOME SWEET HOME
pages 86 and 87

Girl 1 has bed *B*.
Girl 2 has bed *C*.
Girl 3 has bed *A*.
Girl 4 has bed *D*.